W9-AYO-248

| DATE DUE | | | |
|---|---|---|---|
| JE 18'91 | | | |
| DEC 11 '93 | | | |
| 1/10/94 | | | |
| MAY 30 '95 | | | |
| AP 23'01 | | | |
| FE 16'06 | | | |
| | | | |
| | | | |
| | | | |
| | | | |
| | | | |

# cooking the AFRICAN way

**Seafood is a main ingredient in both egusi soup** *(front)* **and fresh fish pepper soup** *(back left)***. Egusi soup is often eaten with fufu** *(back right)***. (Recipes on pages 18, 28, and 29.)**

# cooking the
# AFRICAN way

CONSTANCE NABWIRE &
BERTHA VINING MONTGOMERY

PHOTOGRAPHS BY ROBERT L. & DIANE WOLFE

**easy menu** *ethnic* **cookbooks**

Lerner Publications Company ▪ Minneapolis

**Editor: Vicki Revsbech**
**Drawings by Jeanette Swofford**
**Map by J. Michael Roy**

Additional photographs are reproduced through the courtesy of Hans Olaf Pfannkuch, p. 9; Jim Hathaway, p. 11.

The page border for this book is based on a sunburst pattern found in African art and fabrics.

*To my loving and supportive mother, Mary Alice Vining, and my daughter, Tiffany Elise—B.V.M.*

*This book is for my mother, my family, and my friends who enjoy my cooking—C.N.*

Library of Congress Cataloging-in-Publication Data

Nabwire, Constance R.
    Cooking the African Way.

    (Easy menu ethnic cookbooks)
    Includes index.
    Summary: An introduction to the cooking of East and West Africa, with information on the land and people of this area of the giant continent, and including recipes.
    1. Cookery, African—Juvenile literature. 2. Africa—Social life and customs—Juvenile literature. [1. Cookery, African. 2. Africa, Social life and customs]
I. Montgomery, Bertha Vining. II. Revsbech, Vicki.
III. Wolfe, Robert L., ill. IV. Wolfe, Diane, ill.
V. Swofford, Jeanette, ill. VI. Title VII. Series.
TX725.A4N33    1988        394.1'2'096        88-8877
ISBN 0-8225-0919-9 (lib. bdg.)

Manufactured in the United States of America

1  2  3  4  5  6  7  8  9  10  97  96  95  94  93  92  91  90  89  88

**Bright red tomatoes add color and flavor to fruit salad *(left)* and greens with coconut milk *(right)*. (Recipes on pages 25 and 26.)**

# CONTENTS

West Africa

East Africa

*Peanuts*

*Rice*

Niger River

*Cassava*

*Yams*

*Peanuts*

Dakar ★ SENEGAL
GAMBIA

*Cattle*
BURKINA FASO

*Rice*

*Cattle*

NIGERIA

*Cattle*

*Coffee*

GUINEA-BISSAU

GUINEA

BENIN

*Goats*

Addis Ababa ★

*Sheep*

*Bananas*

SIERRA LEONE

IVORY
COAST

T
O
G
O

GHANA

★ Lagos

*Sheep*

ETHIOPIA

LIBERIA

*Tea*

*Rice*

Accra

★

*Coffee*

UGANDA

*Cattle*

*Goats*

*Bananas*

*Corn*

Kampala ★

KENYA

*Coffee*

Lake
Victoria

★ Nairobi

*Coffee*

*Coffee*

*Goats*

*Sheep*

A
F
R
I
C
A

Red Sea

Atlantic Ocean

Indian Ocean

*Goats*

TANZANIA

Lake Tanganyika

*Cattle*

★ Dar es Salaam

*Tea*

# INTRODUCTION

What do you think of as a typical African dish? Lamb curry from South Africa? Couscous from Tunisia? Peanut soup from Nigeria? African cuisine includes all these foods and many more. The African continent is so vast and is home to so many different kinds of people, that it is difficult to characterize anything as "typically African." This book concentrates on the cooking of East and West Africa.

# THE LAND

West Africa is a cluster of countries along the coast of the South Atlantic Ocean. The countries that make up East Africa lie on the opposite side of the continent and border on the Indian Ocean and the Red Sea. Together, East and West Africa include 16 countries and cover over two million square miles, an area nearly the size of the continent of Australia.

West Africa stretches from Senegal to Nigeria, and all but one country—Burkina Faso—touches on the Atlantic Ocean. The land is low and flat. Some of it is covered with forests, while other parts are made up of grassy plains called savannas. The climate is nearly constant across all of West Africa. There is a region on the coasts of Ghana, Ivory Coast, Liberia, and Sierra Leone that is hot, humid, and rainy all year long. The rest of West Africa is also hot throughout the year but has both a wet and a dry season.

The land of East Africa is far more varied than that of West Africa. East Africa has soaring mountains and steep valleys, thick forests, barren deserts, and fertile highlands.

It contains the highest mountain in Africa—Mount Kilimanjaro—which is located in northeastern Tanzania. Lake Victoria, the second largest lake in the world, can be found on the borders of Uganda, Kenya, and Tanzania.

The climate of East Africa, like the land, is also quite varied. Because the equator runs through the countries of Kenya and Uganda, it is not surprising that most of East Africa is hot year round. There are also highland areas that stay quite cool—often below 50° F—as well as mountains that are tall enough to be snowcapped. Rainfall is uneven across this part of Africa. Some areas have seasons of nearly constant rain, while others receive almost none at all. Drought has been a problem, especially in Ethiopia, where lack of rain has led to serious food shortages.

## THE PEOPLE

Africa is home to people of many different backgrounds including black African, East Indian, Dutch, and Arab. There is a tremendous variety of people living in East and West Africa. Although most East and West Africans are black, they are further divided into hundreds of ethnic groups, or tribes, each with its own language and traditions.

The lives of East and West Africans vary greatly depending on whether they live in the city or the country. Those who live in rural areas—about three-fourths of the total population—have lives that are very much the same as those of their ancestors. They usually live in villages with other people of the same ethnic group. While some villages have houses made of modern materials such as cement and metal, many people still live in houses made of clay or dried mud with roofs of grass or palm leaves.

The people of an African village depend on each other like an extended family. In fact, it is not unusual for everyone in a village to be related in one way or another. Traditionally, the men are responsible for farming the land that surrounds the village. The women help with the farm work and also cook and take care of the children. Even the children have their role in the life of the village. They learn at an early age to help the adults whenever they can until they are old enough to take on adult responsibilities.

Villages very seldom have modern machines or tools for cooking or farming. Plowing is done with a wooden plow pulled by oxen. Food is prepared with the same kinds of hand tools that have been used in Africa for hundreds of years.

One traditional cooking tool found in nearly every East and West African home is the mortar and pestle. A pestle is a club-shaped utensil that is used with a mortar, a sturdy bowl, to grind or pound foods. Another essential tool is the sifter, a square or round utensil with a fine wire mesh across the bottom. It is used to remove small particles from larger pieces of food. The most important "tool" used in traditional African cooking is fire. While stoves are used in the cities, where there is gas and electricity, most East and West Africans still cook over a fire, just as their ancestors did.

There is another side to life in East and West Africa. Every year, an increasing number of people move to large cities such as Lagos, Nigeria, and Addis Ababa, Ethiopia. These cities, with their tall buildings and modern industry, offer a faster-paced, more Westernized lifestyle than can be found in the villages.

**A mortar and pestle can be very small or quite large like this one being used by these women from Senegal.**

## THE FOOD

Because food is sometimes scarce in certain parts of Africa, East and West African cooks have learned to work with whatever they have. African dishes are versatile enough that if a certain ingredient is not available, it is always possible to substitute another or leave it out.

While some people in East and West Africa have started to follow the Western tradition of eating three meals a day, including a large, hearty breakfast, most East and West Africans eat only twice a day. The two meals are eaten at noon and in the evening.

Whether served at noon or at night, an East or West African meal is likely to be made up of a thick stew or soup and a starch. The stew or soup usually contains a variety of vegetables and maybe a little meat, poultry, or fish. The starch can be anything from bread to rice to fufu—which is made by pounding starchy grains and vegetables such as millet, yams, or plantains to a flour and boiling them to a paste. In West Africa, the stew and the starch are often combined to make a one-pot meal such as jollof rice.

When serving a typical East or West African meal, the main dish is placed on individual plates and the starch is served on a communal plate. The diners break off a piece of bread or scoop up a small amount of fufu in their fingers and use it to scoop up some of the food on their plate. The starch cools the heat of the main dish, which can be quite spicy.

East and West Africans may eat only two meals per day, but they snack all day long. A snack might be a piece of bread such as a chapati, roasted or fried plantains, or meat on a stick. In the cities, these and other snack foods are sold on the street. It is unusual to eat something sweet for a snack, except perhaps for a piece of fruit or a doughnut.

Because very few people have refrigeration, the cooking of East and West Africa is based on fresh foods. In the villages, people grow all of their own fruits and vegetables in small gardens. Although the people who live in the cities may have refrigeration and rely somewhat on canned foods, they are still likely to visit the market every day for fresh fruits and vegetables.

This Nigerian woman is selling fruit from an open-market stand.

The variety of fruits and vegetables found in Africa is staggering. Among the gardens and farms of Africa are 90 percent of all the cultivated plants in the world. There are familiar foods such as bananas, oranges, cabbages, and cucumbers as well as the less familiar tamarinds, star apples, plantains, and cassavas. It is hard to believe that the vast majority of these plants were introduced to Africa by the Europeans and Arabs. Among the few plants used for food that are native to the continent are oil palm, millet, and sorghum.

Meat, fish, and poultry are less abundant, and therefore more expensive than fruits and vegetables. One reason that soups and stews are such staples in East and West Africa is that they make a little meat stretch to feed many people. It is not unusual for a meal to contain no meat at all. On the coasts or near large lakes, fish is cheaper than meat, and people often combine meat with fish in the same dish. Chicken is usually saved for guests or special occasions. Meat, poultry, and fish, like fruits and vegetables, are usually served fresh, although they are sometimes preserved by smoking or drying.

To this day, most East and West African cooks do not use recipes when cooking. In fact, until recently it was considered a disgrace in some areas of East and West Africa to write down recipes. Instead, they were passed down from generation to generation strictly by memory.

The recipes in this book were collected from women from different countries all over East and West Africa and then adapted to American measuring standards. A few of the recipes have been changed slightly to suit Western tastes. For instance, fufu is traditionally made with pounded yams or plantains, and some recipes would contain less meat if prepared in Africa. For the most part, however, the recipes are authentic. Once you have had a taste of African cooking, you might try varying the meats and vegetables, making up your own combinations.

# BEFORE YOU BEGIN

Cooking any dish, plain or fancy, is easier and more fun if you are familiar with its ingredients. African cooking makes use of some ingredients that you may not know. You should also be familiar with the special terms that will be used in various recipes in this book. Therefore, *before* you start cooking any of the dishes in this book, study the following "dictionary" of special ingredients and terms very carefully. Then read through each recipe you want to try from beginning to end.

Now you are ready to shop for ingredients and to organize the cookware you will need. Once you have assembled everything, you can begin to cook. It is also very important to read *The Careful Cook* on page 44 before you start. Following these rules will make your cooking experience safe, fun, and easy.

## COOKING UTENSILS

*colander*—A bowl with holes in the bottom and sides. It is used for draining liquid from a solid food.

*pastry brush*—A small brush with nylon bristles used for coating food with melted butter or other liquids

*rolling pin*—A cylindrical tool used for rolling out dough

*skewer*—A thin metal rod used to hold small pieces of food for broiling or grilling

*slotted spoon*—A spoon with small openings in the bowl. It is used to pick solid food out of a liquid.

*spatula*—A flat, thin utensil, usually metal, used to lift, toss, turn, or scoop up food

*tongs*—A utensil shaped either like a scissors or a tweezers with flat, blunt ends used to grasp food

## COOKING TERMS

*brown*—To cook food quickly in fat over high heat so that the surface turns an even brown

*garnish*—To decorate with a small piece of food such as parsley

*sauté*—To fry quickly over high heat in oil or fat, stirring or turning the food to prevent burning

*simmer*—To cook over low heat in liquid kept just below its boiling point. Bubbles may occasionally rise to the surface.

*stir-fry*—To quickly cook bite-size pieces of food in a small amount of oil over high heat

## SPECIAL INGREDIENTS

*black-eyed peas*—Small, tan peas with a large black spot from which they get their name

*bouillon cubes*—Small cubes that make meat broth when combined with hot water

*cardamom*—A spice of the ginger family, used whole or ground, that has a rich aroma and gives food a sweet, cool taste

*chili*—Small, hot red or green pepper

*cloves*—Dried buds from a small evergreen tree that can be used whole or ground to flavor food

*coconut milk*—The white, milky liquid extracted from coconut meat, used to give a coconut flavor to foods. It is available at oriental groceries.

*collard greens*—The leaves of a plant related to the cabbage

*coriander*—An herb used ground or fresh as a flavoring or garnish

*cumin*—The seeds of an herb used whole or ground to give food a pungent, slightly hot flavor *eggplant*—A vegetable with shiny purple-black skin and yellow flesh

*egg roll skins*—Thin sheets of dough that can be wrapped around a filling and fried

*egusi seeds*—Melon seeds with a pleasant nutty flavor

*garlic*—An herb whose distinctive flavor is used in many dishes. Each bulb can be broken up into several sections called cloves. Most recipes use only one or two cloves. Before you chop up a clove of garlic, you will have to remove the papery covering that surrounds it.

*ginger root*—A knobby, light brown root used to flavor foods

*jalapeño pepper*—Mexican hot peppers

*mango*—A greenish-yellow tropical fruit with soft, juicy yellow flesh

*mung bean*—A bean often used in oriental cooking that is available in oriental grocery stores

*paprika*—Dried ground sweet red peppers used for its flavor and its red color

*plantain*—A starchy fruit that looks like a banana and must be cooked before it is eaten

*seasoned salt*—A commercially prepared mixture of salt and other seasonings

*thyme*—A fragrant herb used fresh or dried to season food

*turmeric*—A yellow, aromatic spice made from the root of the turmeric plant

*vermicelli*—Pasta made in long, thin strands that are thinner than spaghetti

*yeast*—An ingredient used in cooking to make bread rise and cause liquid to ferment

# AN AFRICAN MENU

East and West Africans traditionally eat two meals per day, one at noon and one in the evening. The two meals are basically the same. They are usually made up of a soup or stew served with some sort of starch such as fufu or chapatis. In the cities, more and more people are eating three meals per day—breakfast, lunch, and dinner—rather than the traditional two. Desserts are also more common in the city than they are in rural villages. Below is a West African menu and an East African menu, followed by suggestions for how to combine foods from the east and the west.   *Recipe included in book*

## AN EAST AFRICAN MENU

### I
*Chapatis
*Groundnut sauce
*Vegetable casserole

### II
Rice
*Fresh steamed fish

### III
Rice
*Greens with coconut milk
*Luku

### IV
*Chapatis
*Meat curry
*Choroko sauce
*Vermicelli and raisins

## A WEST AFRICAN MENU

### I
*Fufu
*Egusi soup
Fruit

### II
*Jollof rice
*Baked plantain on the shell

### III
*Grilled plantains
*Fresh fish pepper soup

### IV
*Fufu
*Spinach stew
*Fruit salad

## AN EAST AND WEST AFRICAN MENU

**Breakfast**

I

| *Rice pancakes | East African |
| Fruit topping | |

II

| *Chapatis | East African |
| Tea | |

**Lunch**

I

| *Fruit salad | West African |
| *Choroko sauce | East African |
| *Chapatis | East African |
| *Sweet balls | West African |

II

| Rice | |
| *Meat on a stick | East African |
| *Fruit salad | West African |

**Dinner**

I

| *Samusas | East African |
| *Boiled plantains | East and West African |
| *Spinach stew | West African |
| *Vermicelli and raisins | East African |

II

| *Akara | West African |
| *Greens with coconut milk | East African |
| *Groundnut sauce | East and West African |
| Rice | |
| *Fresh steamed fish | East African |
| *Baked plantain on the shell | East and West African |

# BREADS AND STAPLES

Mild-flavored breads and such staples as fufu or rice are natural accompaniments to Africa's hearty and spicy soups, stews, and sauces. These foods are often used as "utensils" to scoop up other foods, and some, such as chapatis, can also be eaten alone as a snack.

# Fufu
## West Africa

*Fufu is a West African staple that is eaten with soups and stews. This is an Americanized version of fufu. To give your fufu a more authentic flavor, try leaving out the margarine and the salt.*

**4 cups water**
**1¼ cups Cream of Wheat®**
**1 cup potato flakes**
**1 tablespoon margarine (optional)**
**⅛ teaspoon salt (optional)**

1. In a small saucepan, bring 2 cups water to a boil over medium heat. Reduce heat to low.
2. In a large saucepan, bring 2 cups water to a boil over high heat. Reduce heat to medium and add Cream of Wheat® ¼ cup at a time, stirring constantly. Add tablespoons of hot water from the other pan when mixture gets too thick to stir.
3. Add potato flakes ¼ cup at a time, stirring constantly and, when necessary, adding hot water.
4. Add margarine and salt and stir until margarine is melted. Continue to cook, stirring vigorously, until fufu pulls away from the sides of the pan and forms a ball.
5. Form fufu into cup-size balls and place on plates or in bowls.

*Makes about 3 cups fufu*

# Chapatis
## Kenya, Tanzania, Uganda

*In Africa, chapatis are considered to be a luxury, because only those who can afford to buy imported flour can make them.*

½ **teaspoon salt**
**3 cups unbleached all-purpose flour**
¾ **cup plus 1 to 3 tablespoons**
    **vegetable oil**
¾ **to 1 cup water**

1. In a large bowl, combine salt and 2½ cups flour. Add ¾ cup oil and mix well. Add water little by little, stirring after each addition, until dough is soft. Knead dough in bowl for 5 to 10 minutes.

2. Sprinkle about ¼ cup flour on a flat surface. Take a 2-inch ball of dough and, with a floured rolling pin, roll out into a ⅛-inch-thick circle the size of a saucer. Repeat with remaining dough, sprinkling flat surface with flour if dough sticks.

3. Heat 1 tablespoon oil over medium-high heat for 1 minute. Fry chapati 3 to 5 minutes per side or until brown.

4. Remove from pan and let drain on paper towels. Fry remaining chapatis, adding more oil if necessary.

5. Serve immediately or place in a covered container until ready to serve.

*Makes 6 chapatis*

Rice pancakes *(front)* and chapatis *(back)* can be served with stew or alone as a snack. Chapatis are delicious with butter or sprinkled with sugar, and rice pancakes are often eaten with jam.

# Rice Pancakes
## *Kenya*

*The addition of yeast makes these pancakes light and airy. If the yeast does not start to foam after about 5 minutes in warm water, throw it out and try again with new yeast.*

1 teaspoon active dry yeast
½ to 1 cup warm water (105 to 115° F)
1 cup sugar
2¾ cups rice flour
¼ teaspoon ground cardamom
¼ cup canned coconut milk
½ cup vegetable oil

1. In a small bowl, dissolve yeast in ½ cup warm water. Add a pinch of sugar and set aside in a warm place for about 5 minutes or until yeast mixture foams.
2. In a large bowl, combine sugar, flour, and cardamom. Add coconut milk and yeast mixture and stir. Mixture should have the consistency of pancake batter.

If too thick, stir in water little by little until batter runs slowly from spoon.
3. Cover bowl with a towel (not terry cloth) and set aside in a warm place for about 1 hour or until mixture nearly doubles in size.
4. Heat 1 tablespoon oil over medium-high heat for 1 minute.
5. Pour ½ cup of batter into pan and spread with a spoon to form a pancake about the size of a saucer. Cover pan and cook for 1 to 2 minutes or until golden brown on bottom. Sprinkle pancake with a few drops of oil and turn over with a spatula. Cover and cook for another 1 to 2 minutes or until golden brown on other side. Repeat with remaining batter, adding more oil when necessary.
6. Serve hot.

*Makes about 10 pancakes*

# SNACKS AND APPETIZERS

Although Africans traditionally eat only two meals a day, one in the late morning and one in the late evening, they eat many snacks throughout the day. These snacks, which can also be served as appetizers, are usually very nutritious and actually amount to "mini-meals."

## Meat on a Stick
### *Ethiopia, Uganda*

*The seasoned meat and onions can also be cooked in a frying pan with a little vegetable oil. In Africa, the skewers are cooked over hot coals.*

**1 teaspoon ground red pepper**
**1 teaspoon garlic powder**
**½ teaspoon seasoned salt**
**1½ pounds beef tenderloin or round steak, cut into bite-size pieces**
**1 medium onion, peeled and cut into 1-inch pieces**

1. Combine red pepper, garlic powder, and seasoned salt in a wide, shallow bowl. Add beef and mix with hands to coat with spices.
2. Preheat broiler.
3. Thread beef and onion pieces onto 12-inch skewers. Broil 4 to 5 minutes per side or until meat is tender.

*Makes 8 skewers*

**African cuisine offers a wide variety of snacks and appetizers including meat on a stick** *(front)*, **akara** *(back left)*, **and samusas** *(back right).*

# Samusas
## *East Africa*

*This snack, which originated in India,
is a favorite in East Africa. In the cities,
samusas are sold at street stands.*

1½ **pounds extra-lean ground beef**
½ **teaspoon cumin seed**
2 **tablespoons chopped green onion**
  **dash garlic powder**
  **dash seasoned salt**
  **dash black pepper**
¼ **cup all-purpose flour**
2 **teaspoons water**
1 **package square egg roll skins**
1 **cup vegetable oil**

1. In a large frying pan, mash ground beef
with a fork. Add cumin, green onion,
garlic powder, seasoned salt, and black
pepper and mix well.
2. Brown meat over medium heat. Drain
off fat and set meat aside.
3. In a small bowl, combine flour and 2
teaspoons water and stir to make a paste.

4. Place 1 egg roll skin on a flat surface.
Cover remaining skins with a slightly
damp kitchen towel (not terry cloth) so
they don't dry out. Fill according to direc-
tions that follow recipe.
5. In a large frying pan, heat oil over
medium-high heat for 4 to 5 minutes. With
tongs, carefully place 1 samusa in oil.
Samusa should fry to golden brown in
about 3 minutes. If it takes longer than
this, increase the temperature of the oil.
Remove from oil with slotted spoon and
drain on paper towels. Repeat with remaining samusas, frying 3 or 4 at a time.
*Makes about 24 samusas*

HOW TO FILL SAMUSAS
1. With a pastry brush, brush all 4 edges
of skin with flour and water mixture.
2. Place about 1 tablespoon of meat mixture just above center of skin.
3. Fold skin in half over filling to form a
triangle and press edges together to seal.
4. Repeat with remaining skins.

# Akara

## *Nigeria*

*This appetizer is often eaten with a sweetened custard.*

**1 cup dried black-eyed peas**
**⅓ to ½ cup water**
**½ cup finely chopped onions**
**¼ teaspoon black pepper**
**½ teaspoon salt**
**½ teaspoon chopped and seeded chili**
      **or ¼ teaspoon ground red pepper**
**1 egg**
      **vegetable oil**

1. Place the peas in a large kettle and cover with water. Let soak for a few hours or overnight.
2. With your hands under water, rub peas together between your palms to remove skins. Skins will float to the top and can be skimmed off.
3. Drain peas in a colander. Place peas in a blender or food processor with ⅓ cup water and blend for about 20 seconds or until smooth.
4. Place ground peas in a large bowl. If mixture is dry, stir in water little by little until pasty.
5. Add remaining ingredients except for oil and beat with a spoon until light and airy.
6. In a large frying pan, heat 1 inch oil over medium heat for 4 to 5 minutes or until temperature measures 375°. Carefully drop teaspoons of dough into oil and fry about 5 minutes or until golden brown.
7. Remove akara from oil with slotted spoon and drain on paper towel. Serve immediately.

*Serves 6*

# FRUITS AND VEGETABLES

Hundreds of varieties of fruits and vegetables grow in Africa, and they are an important part of African cooking. What people don't grow in their own gardens, they buy in open-air markets that offer everything from bananas and cucumbers to guavas and yams. These fruit and vegetable dishes can be eaten alone for a snack or a light lunch or supper or served as side dishes.

## Fruit Salad
### *Nigeria*

*This salad is usually only served in well-to-do households or for special occasions. Chunks of papaya can also be added.*

**4 to 6 large, ripe mangoes**
**4 medium bananas**
**1 large tomato (optional)**
**1 cup cubed pineapple**
   **juice from 1 medium lime**
**1 cup water**
**½ cup sugar**
**½ cup shredded coconut for garnish**

1. Wash and peel mangoes. Cut into bite-size cubes. Peel and slice bananas. Cut tomato in half, remove seeds, and cut into cubes.
2. Combine mangoes, bananas, tomatoes, and pineapple in a large bowl and toss, being careful not to mash fruit.
3. In a small bowl, combine lime juice, 1 cup water, and sugar and stir well.
4. Pour dressing over fruit, cover, and refrigerate for at least 1 hour. Toss well before serving. Garnish with shredded coconut.

*Serves 4 to 6*

# Greens with Coconut Milk

## Kenya, Uganda

*Other types of greens, such as spinach, turnip greens, or kale, can be substituted for the collard greens.*

**¾ cup water**
**1 pound fresh collard greens, cleaned and chopped, or 1 10-ounce package frozen chopped collard greens, thawed**
**1 medium onion, peeled and chopped**
**3 large tomatoes, cubed**
**1 cup canned coconut milk**
**dash of salt**

1. In a large saucepan, bring ¾ cup water to a boil over high heat. Add collard greens, reduce heat to low, and simmer for 4 to 5 minutes.
2. Add onions, tomatoes, coconut milk, and salt and stir well. Cook, uncovered, 20 minutes more. Serve hot.

*Serves 4 to 6*

# Versatile Plantain

## East and West Africa

*Plantains are an important food in both East and West Africa. Although it is a member of the banana family, the plantain is often served as a vegetable. For variety, try adding tomatoes, onions, fresh spinach, or a dash of curry powder to boiled plantains.*

**Fried Plantains:**

**3 large, ripe plantains**
**vegetable oil**

1. Peel plantains and slice into thin rounds.
2. In a large frying pan, heat ¼ inch oil over medium-high heat for 4 to 5 minutes.
3. Add plantain slices and fry for 4 to 5 minutes or until golden brown on both sides.
4. Remove from oil with slotted spoon and drain on paper towel.

## Boiled Plantains:

**2 large, firm green plantains**
   **dash salt**
   **butter**

1. Peel plantains and cut into 1-inch pieces. Place in a large kettle.
2. Cover with water and add salt.
3. Bring to a boil over high heat. Reduce heat to medium-low, cover, and simmer for 10 minutes or until plantain can be pierced with a fork. Serve hot with butter.

## Grilled Plantains:

**2 or 3 large, ripe plantains**

1. Cut plantains in half lengthwise and widthwise. Do not peel.
2. Preheat broiler.
3. Grill or broil, skin side down, for 5 to 7 minutes or until plantain can be easily pierced with a fork and isn't sticky.
4. When cool enough to handle, peel plantain and serve.

*Each recipe serves 4*

**Plantains are a versatile fruit that can be served fried *(front)*, boiled with other vegetables *(back left)*, or grilled *(back right)*.**

# SOUPS AND SAUCES

African soups and sauces are quite similar to each other. Soups are served with a starch such as fufu on the side for dipping, while sauces, which are thicker than soups, are often served over a starch such as rice.

## Fresh Fish Pepper Soup
### West Africa

*The combination of fish and hot peppers is very typical of West African cooking.*

**2 pounds firm white boneless fish, cut into bite-size pieces**
**4 cups water**
**2 tomatoes**
**1 onion, peeled**
**3 to 4 sprigs fresh parsley or 1 teaspoon dried parsley**
**2 chilies or jalapeño peppers, seeded**
**2 teaspoons salt**
**1 teaspoon dried thyme**

1. Wash fish, place in large saucepan, and add 4 cups water.
2. Finely chop tomatoes, onion, parsley, and peppers and add to water. Add salt and thyme and stir.
3. Bring mixture to a boil over high heat. Reduce heat to low, cover, and simmer for 20 minutes or until fish is tender.
4. Serve immediately.

*Serves 4 to 6*

# Egusi Soup
## *Nigeria*

*Ground egusi seeds give this soup a unique color and flavor. If you can't find egusi seeds, you can substitute pumpkin seeds. Drained smoked oysters and chicken can be used in place of the crab and the beef.*

¾ **cup egusi seeds**
1½ **pounds beef tenderloin**
¾ **teaspoon salt**
¼ **teaspoon black pepper**
¼ **cup peanut oil**
2 **large tomatoes, chopped**
1 **small onion, peeled and chopped**
1 **or 2 chilies or jalapeño peppers,
   seeded and chopped**
1 **8-ounce can tomato sauce**
1½ **cups water**
   **any combination of crab, shrimp, or
   smoked fish adding up to 2 pounds**
1 **pound fresh spinach, cleaned and
   finely chopped, or 1 10-ounce
   package frozen chopped spinach,
   thawed**

1. Place egusi seeds in a blender and blend for 30 to 40 seconds or until mixture is a powdery paste. Set aside.
2. Wash beef and cut into bite-size cubes. Season with salt and black pepper.
3. In a large frying pan, heat oil over medium-high heat for 4 to 5 minutes. Add beef and sauté for 3 to 5 minutes or until brown but not cooked through.
4. Place tomatoes, onions, and peppers in a blender and blend for about 30 seconds or until smooth.
5. Add tomato mixture to meat, reduce heat to medium-low, and cover. Cook for 1½ to 2 hours or until meat is tender.
6. Add tomato sauce, 1½ cups water, crab, shrimp, and smoked fish and simmer for 10 minutes.
7. Add spinach and ground egusi seeds and continue to simmer for 10 minutes more. Serve with fufu.

*Serves 6*

# Choroko Sauce

## *Uganda*

*Although the flavor will be different, choroko sauce can also be made with split peas.*

1½ cups dried Shirakiku® brand
     mung beans
2 tablespoons vegetable oil
3 medium tomatoes, cut into bite-size
     pieces
1 large onion, peeled and chopped
3 or 4 cloves garlic, peeled and
     crushed
½ teaspoon seasoned salt
     dash salt
     dash black pepper
½ cup water

1. Place beans in a medium bowl and cover with water. Let soak overnight.
2. Drain beans in a colander.
3. Fill a medium saucepan half full of water and bring to a boil over high heat. Add beans and cook for 1 to 1½ hours or

**Flavorful groundnut sauce *(front)* and choroko sauce *(back)* are rich in protein. They can be served with chapatis or over rice.**

until tender.

4. Drain beans in a colander and place in a medium bowl. Mash well with a fork.

5. In a large frying pan, heat oil over medium heat for 1 minute.

6. Add tomatoes, onions, and garlic and sauté until onions are transparent.

7. Add mashed beans, seasoned salt, salt, black pepper, and ½ cup water and simmer for 15 to 20 minutes. Serve over rice or with chapatis.

*Serves 4 to 6*

# Groundnut Sauce
## East and West Africa

*This sauce is made from groundnuts, better known in some countries as peanuts. Groundnut sauce is often substituted for meat dishes, although it is also served with dried meat and dried fish. This recipe works best if made with natural peanut butter with no sugar added.*

**2 tablespoons vegetable oil**

**1 medium onion, peeled and chopped**
**2 medium tomatoes, cut into bite-size pieces**
**1 small eggplant, with or without peel, cut into bite-size pieces**
**½ cup smooth peanut butter**
**¼ cup water**

1. In a large frying pan, heat oil over medium heat for 1 minute. Add onions and sauté until transparent.

2. Add tomatoes and cook for 5 minutes. Add eggplant and cook for 5 minutes more.

3. In a small bowl, combine peanut butter and ¼ cup water and stir to make a paste. Add to tomato mixture and stir well.

4. Reduce heat to medium-low and simmer, uncovered, for 10 minutes or until eggplant is tender.

5. Serve with rice, potatoes, sweet potatoes, or plantains.

*Serves 4 to 6*

# MAIN DISHES

In both East and West Africa, a thick, hearty stew is likely to be the main dish at every meal. However, the meat, vegetables, and starch are also occasionally served separately, expecially in East Africa.

## Fresh Steamed Fish
*Uganda*

*In Africa, this dish is made with a whole fish, with or without the head. This recipe works well with red snapper or orange roughy.*

¼ **cup vegetable oil**
2 **medium onions, peeled and chopped**
1 **clove garlic, peeled and chopped**
3 **medium tomatoes, chopped**
½ **teaspoon salt**
¼ **teaspoon black pepper**
2 **pounds fish fillets**

1. In a large frying pan, heat oil over medium heat for 1 minute. Add onions and sauté until transparent.
2. Add garlic, tomatoes, salt, and black pepper and mix well.
3. Place fish in the center of tomato mixture. Cover and simmer for about 25 minutes or until fish is tender and flaky.

*Serves 4 to 6*

**Fresh steamed fish** *(front)* **and vegetable casserole** *(back)* **are two dishes that take advantage of the fresh ingredients so important to African cooking.**

# Vegetable Casserole
## *Uganda*

*The variations possible with this colorful vegetable casserole are endless. Either make it with the vegetables listed here or substitute your own favorites.*

**2 tablespoons vegetable oil**
**1 small onion, sliced and separated**
    **into rings**
**1 medium eggplant, unpeeled, cut into**
    **bite-size pieces**
**1 small sweet red pepper, cored and**
    **thinly sliced**
**1 or 2 cloves garlic, peeled and crushed**
**1 pound fresh spinach, cleaned and**
    **chopped, or 1 10-ounce package**
    **frozen chopped spinach, thawed**
**1 small zucchini, peeled and sliced**
**2 medium tomatoes, cut in wedges**
**½ teaspoon salt**
**¼ teaspoon black pepper**

1. In a large frying pan, heat oil over medium-high heat for 4 to 5 minutes.
2. Add onions to pan and stir-fry for 2 to 3 minutes. Continue to add vegetables to pan in order listed, stir-frying each 2 to 3 minutes before adding the next.
3. Stir in salt and black pepper. Cover pan, reduce heat to low, and simmer 10 to 15 minutes or until vegetables are tender.
4. Serve immediately.

*Serves 4 to 6*

# Jollof Rice
## West Africa

*Jollof rice is a well-known West African dish. It can be made with chicken or beef or no meat at all.*

**4 to 6 pieces chicken**
**½ teaspoon salt**
**¼ teaspoon black pepper**
**¼ cup vegetable oil**
**1 medium onion, peeled and finely chopped**
**¼ pound cubed salt pork or ham**
**2 cubes beef bouillon**
**¼ teaspoon ground red pepper**
**½ teaspoon dried thyme or 1 sprig fresh thyme, crushed**
**1½ cups water**
**1 6-ounce can tomato paste**
**1¼ cups uncooked rice**
**any combination of green peas or chopped string beans, carrots, green pepper or tomatoes adding up to 2 cups**

1. Season chicken with salt and black pepper. In a large frying pan, heat oil over medium-high heat for 4 to 5 minutes. Add chicken pieces and brown on both sides.
2. Place chicken in a kettle and set aside. Add onions and salt pork to oil in frying pan and sauté until onions are transparent. Add onions and pork to kettle. Set frying pan aside. (Do not discard oil.)
3. Add bouillon cubes, red pepper, thyme, 1½ cups water, and tomato paste to kettle and stir well. Simmer over low heat for about 10 minutes.
4. Add rice to frying pan and stir to coat with oil. Add rice and vegetables to kettle, stir well, and cover. Cook over low heat 35 to 40 minutes or until vegetables and rice are tender.

*Serves 4 to 6*

# Spinach Stew
## *Ghana*

*This is a very quick, economical meal for city dwellers in Africa, who have easy access to convenient canned and frozen foods. Spinach stew takes little time to prepare and is very nutritious.*

**¾ cup vegetable oil**
**1 small onion, peeled and cubed**
**1 small tomato, cubed**
**3 ounces tomato paste**
**1 pound fresh spinach, cleaned and chopped, or 1 10-ounce package frozen chopped spinach, thawed**
**1 12-ounce can corned beef**
**1 teaspoon ground red pepper**
**1 teaspoon salt**

1. In a large frying pan, heat oil over medium heat for 1 minute. Add onions and sauté until transparent.
2. Add tomatoes and tomato paste and cook for 5 minutes. Add remaining ingredients, cover, and cook for 30 to 35 minutes over medium-low heat.
3. Serve over rice.

*Serves 4 to 6*

**Both jollof rice** *(front)* **and spinach stew** *(back)* **are hearty enough to be served alone for a satisfying lunch or supper.**

# Luku
## Ethiopia

*Because of the high cost of chicken in Africa, luku is usually reserved for special occasions or celebrations.*

**8 hard-boiled eggs**
**¾ cup vegetable oil**
**5 to 6 cups chopped onion**
**¼ cup tomato paste**
**½ cup water**
**2 teaspoons salt**
**¾ teaspoon black pepper**
**1¼ tablespoons finely chopped garlic**
**2 teaspoons paprika**
**¼ teaspoon ground cumin (optional)**
**8 pieces chicken**

1. Remove shells from eggs. With a sharp knife, make 4 to 5 shallow cuts on both sides of each egg. Set aside.
2. In a large kettle, heat 2 tablespoons oil over medium-high heat for 1 minute. Add onions and sauté for 8 to 10 minutes or until onions start to turn brown.

3. Reduce heat to medium and add tomato paste and ½ cup water. Stir well. Cook for 10 minutes, then add remaining oil. Cook for 5 minutes more.
4. Add salt, black pepper, garlic, paprika, cumin, and chicken. Reduce heat to low and simmer, uncovered, for about 30 minutes.
5. Add eggs, cover, and cook for 10 minutes or until chicken is tender.

*Serves 6*

Luku *(left)* and meat curry *(right)* are two spicy dishes that are typically Ethiopian.

# Meat Curry
## *Ethiopia*

*Curries are very popular in Ethiopia. This dish is sometimes made with lamb or goat.*

½ cup vegetable oil
½ cup plus 2 tablespoons chopped
    onion
4 cloves garlic, peeled and finely
    chopped
1 1-inch piece ginger root, cut in half
2 teaspoons cumin seed
4 whole cardamom seeds
1 cinnamon stick
4 whole cloves
½ teaspoon ground red pepper
1 teaspoon turmeric
6 ounces tomato paste
4 to 6 pieces chicken
2 medium white potatoes, peeled and
    quartered
½ cup fresh coriander

1. In a large frying pan, heat oil over medium heat for 1 minute. Add onion, garlic, ginger root, cumin, cardamom, cinnamon stick, cloves, red pepper, and turmeric and stir.
2. Stir in tomato paste and cook about 10 minutes or until tomato paste separates from oil. Stir to blend oil and tomato paste.
3. Add chicken, reduce heat to low, and cover. Simmer for 35 minutes.
4. Add potatoes, cover, and simmer 15 minutes or until tender.
5. Add coriander and simmer, uncovered, 10 minutes more.

*Serves 4 to 6*

# DESSERTS

Sweets have not traditionally been part of the African diet. While there is more interest in desserts today than there used to be, an African meal is still far more likely to be followed by a piece of fresh fruit, such as an orange or a mango, than any sort of cake or pie. The following desserts are typically African because none of them is too rich or too sweet.

# Baked Plantain on the Shell
## East and West Africa

*This recipe is an easy way to enjoy an exotic fruit.*

**4 large, ripe plantains**
**½ cup brown sugar**
**¾ teaspoon cinnamon**
**¼ cup butter or margarine, melted**

1. Preheat oven to 350°.
2. Wash plantains and cut in half lengthwise. Do not peel.
3. Arrange in a shallow baking dish with cut sides facing up.
4. In a small bowl, combine brown sugar, cinnamon, and melted butter and stir well.
5. Top plantains with brown sugar mixture.
6. Cover pan and bake for 35 minutes or until plantains are soft.

*Serves 4*

**Like most African desserts, vermicelli and raisins *(front)*, plantain on the shell *(back left)*, and sweet balls *(back right)* are light and tasty and not very sweet.**

# Vermicelli and Raisins
## *Kenya*

*If you leave out the dates and nuts, increase the amount of raisins by ½ cup.*

**2 tablespoons vegetable oil**
**2 cups vermicelli, broken into 1-inch**
    **pieces**
**2 cups hot water**
**¾ teaspoon ground cardamom**
**¼ cup sugar**
**¼ cup raisins**
**¼ cup chopped dates (optional)**
**¼ cup chopped walnuts (optional)**

1. In a large frying pan, heat oil over medium heat for 1 minute. Add vermicelli and sauté until light brown.
2. Slowly add 2 cups hot water. Stir in cardamom, sugar, raisins, dates, and nuts.
3. Cover, reduce heat to low, and simmer over medium-low heat, stirring occasionally, for about 10 minutes or until all water is absorbed and vermicelli is tender.

*Serves 4 to 6*

# Sweet Balls

## *Ghana*

*These little doughnuts are best when they are still warm.*

1 egg
½ teaspoon salt
3 tablespoons baking powder
1½ cups sugar
½ teaspoon nutmeg
1½ cups warm water
3¾ to 4¼ cups all-purpose flour
    vegetable oil

1. In a large bowl, combine egg, salt, baking powder, sugar, and nutmeg and stir well. Add 1½ cups warm water and stir again.
2. Gradually stir in enough flour so that dough is stiff and only slightly sticky.
3. With clean, floured hands, roll dough into balls the size of walnuts.
4. Pour ½ inch oil into pan and heat over medium-high heat for 4 to 5 minutes.
5. Carefully place balls in oil, a few at a time, and fry 3 or 4 minutes per side or until golden brown. Remove from pan with slotted spoon and drain on paper towel. Serve warm.

*Makes 25 to 30 doughnuts*

# THE CAREFUL COOK

Whenever you cook, there are certain safety rules you must always keep in mind.

1. Always wash your hands before handling food.
2. Thoroughly wash all raw vegetables and fruits to remove dirt and chemicals.
3. Use a cutting board when cutting up vegetables and fruits. Don't cut them up in your hand! And be sure to cut in a direction *away* from you and your fingers.
4. Long hair or loose clothing can catch fire if brought near the burners of a stove. If you have long hair, tie it back before cooking.
5. Turn all pot handles toward the back of the stove so that you will not catch your sleeves or jewelry on them. This is especially important when younger brothers and sisters are around. They could easily knock off a pot and get burned.
6. Always use a pot holder to steady hot pots or to take pans out of the oven. Don't use a wet cloth on a hot pan because the steam it produces could burn you.

7. Lift the lid of a steaming pot with the opening away from you so that you will not get burned.
8. If you get burned, hold the burn under cold running water. Do not put grease or butter on it. Cold water helps to take the heat out, but grease or butter will only keep it in.
9. If grease or cooking oil catches fire, throw baking soda or salt at the bottom of the flame to put it out. (Water will *not* put out a grease fire.) Call for help, and try to turn all the stove burners to "off."

## HANDLING CHILIES

Fresh chilies have to be handled with care because they contain oils that can burn your eyes or mouth. After working with chilies, be sure not to touch your face until you have washed your hands thoroughly with soap and water. To be extra cautious, wear rubber gloves while fixing chilies. The way you cut the peppers will affect their "hotness." If you take out the seeds, the flavor will be sharp but not fiery. If you leave the seeds in, beware!

# METRIC CONVERSION CHART

| WHEN YOU KNOW | | MULTIPLY BY | TO FIND | |
|---|---|---|---|---|
| MASS (weight) | | | | |
| ounces | (oz) | 28.0 | grams | (g) |
| pounds | (lb) | 0.45 | kilograms | (kg) |
| VOLUME | | | | |
| teaspoons | (tsp) | 5.0 | milliliters | (ml) |
| tablespoons | (Tbsp) | 15.0 | milliliters | |
| fluid ounces | (oz) | 30.0 | milliliters | |
| cup | (c) | 0.24 | liters | (l) |
| pint | (pt) | 0.47 | liters | |
| quart | (qt) | 0.95 | liters | |
| gallon | (gal) | 3.8 | liters | |
| TEMPERATURE | | | | |
| Fahrenheit | (°F) | 5/9 (after | Celsius | (°C) |
| temperature | | subtracting 32) | temperature | |

## COMMON MEASURES AND THEIR EQUIVALENTS

3 teaspoons = 1 tablespoon

8 tablespoons = ½ cup

2 cups = 1 pint

2 pints = 1 quart

4 quarts = 1 gallon

16 ounces = 1 pound

# INDEX

*(recipes indicated by **bold face** type)*

# ABOUT THE AUTHORS

**Bertha Vining Montgomery** grew up in Social Circle, Georgia. She graduated from Spelman College in Georgia with a B.S. in home economics. Montgomery has been an instructor of home economics for the Minneapolis Public Schools since 1968 and has taught in all areas of home economics at both the junior and senior high school levels. She would like to thank Janet Clemetson, Farha Ibrahim, the Lawal family, Rukiya Mahmood, and Uche Iheagwara for their help and encouragement with this book.

**Constance Nabwire** was born and raised in Uganda. She attended King's College Budo in Uganda before coming to the United States on the African Student Program for American Universities. After earning a B.A. in sociology and psychology from Spelman College in Georgia, Nabwire attended the University of Minnesota on a fellowship by the American Association of University Women and was awarded an M.A. in social work. Nabwire is currently a social worker for the Minneapolis Public Schools. She has also published several short stories and articles about her native land. Nabwire would like to thank her friends who contributed their ideas and recipes to this book.

Cooking the **AFRICAN** Way
Cooking the **CARIBBEAN** Way
Cooking the **CHINESE** Way
Cooking the **ENGLISH** Way
Cooking the **FRENCH** Way
Cooking the **GERMAN** Way
Cooking the **GREEK** Way
Cooking the **HUNGARIAN** Way
Cooking the **INDIAN** Way
Cooking the **ISRAELI** Way
Cooking the **ITALIAN** Way
Cooking the **JAPANESE** Way
Cooking the **KOREAN** Way
Cooking the **LEBANESE** Way
Cooking the **MEXICAN** Way
Cooking the **NORWEGIAN** Way
Cooking the **POLISH** Way
Cooking the **RUSSIAN** Way
Cooking the **SPANISH** Way
Cooking the **THAI** Way
Cooking the **VIETNAMESE** Way